Red Ink

Ryan Jones

Table of Contents

Short-term thinkers are destructive to their future.

You will be here before the story ends.

Mercy is speaking another story
over me.

'When I'm older I'll understand'
Those words I'll never understand...

Grace is no longer grace when you've earned it...

I needed a better warning than the one you gave.
I shouldn't have wanted so long.

Are you here? My heart calls; it calls your name.

Dream God Size Dreams...Never.Ever.Give.Up

The Rest
"Part II"

It's much easier said than done but I will
have to change.

You call, never to be late.
How my heart has changed,
never to be the same.

Have tough skin but a soft heart .

I have a unique opportunity. I
can't let it go to waste. I'm
not where I need to be...But
I'm alive! I could do
something...today I have
breath. What will I do with it?

Unsharpened Arrows

So many violets and pinks;
And letters written in red.
But no one to share
The colors in the air.

Much time lived
And little left to spare.
The voices getting louder everywhere.

Small tales
I had to tell.
But they know
I never held.

"So the story begins"

Remember Me

I'm short on words
And desperate to get your attention.
I want to earn your affection;
Be someone you could love for eternity.

What if I fall short?
Stage lights never grace my head?
What if I can't find the one I'm looking for?
Or if I do and it doesn't work out?

Do you know my name among millions who know yours?
Can you find me in crowded city streets?
Will you search until you find me?

If I die will you be waiting on my arrival?
And if you come before I die
Would I be one of the first you find?
Or one of the last you decide to pass?

Whatever it would take for you to notice me;
Remember my face and not just be a name on a page.
Whatever that life is, that's the life I want to live.

What if I do everything I can?
Pray every night to be someone other than me?
What if I end up rich and famous?
Get lost in it and never climb my way out?
What if I stay content and bury a treasure you have given me?
Could I just be a waste of time?
Unfinished and unable?

"My faith should match God's faithfulness."

Secret Place

Much higher than treetops
Do birds dare to fly?
Much further in space
Can human minds dream?

Amazing sight
It's beautiful and bright
Flowers dancing
In heavenly light.

Churches on mountains
I can barely breathe
Most romantic place I've ever seen.
More treasure than earth can store
Secret cities off the ocean's floor

Unspeakable joy
Mystery and freedom
A healing hand
That took pain away
Paid the ultimate price
For me to live in eternity

**"Last night I saw God dancing
in the moonlight."**

What I Really Want to Say

My dreams are mine and are mine to keep. I have been placed in this world by God and it's not a right but a privilege. For all I can be and all I am to be, I pray it's for Him. I must not catch contentment but remain content. I don't own anything I own and will not own what I receive in the future.

I do, however, own my soul and I have decided to give it away. It was better left in the hands that created me and breathe life into me. It is honorable not to hide what I rather others not know and say the words I'm most often scared to say. In that I hope my heart stays pure and my intentions well known. In everything I do let man know where I stand and God take comfort in blessing anything I produce. I have a responsibility every day, to reach the unreachable and to speak the unspeakable. I have a story worth telling, so let it be told.

Acknowledgements

I want to thank my Father for giving me this unique opportunity to write a second book. I want "Red Ink" to advance His Kingdom and be used for His glory. I also want to thank Mom, Dad, Brendan, Kaitlynn, Pops, Jeanne, and of course my lovely Grandma, Gram J, Papa, The Upton's, Sandra, Laura, Willie, Jailee, and Morgan.

Special thanks:

My parents and my best friends Daniel, Savage, Curtis, and Josh.

Anne Landry for being my hero and leading me to Christ; without you there is no God, no high school, no college, no job, and certainly no book.

Brad Waters for buying my all those marketable CD's when I was broke. The dream of getting my work published started with your belief in me.

Writer Evelyn Huckaby for getting my foot in the door; you paved the way for me to get this done.

My great friends Chris Callahan and Ms. Debra for being so supportive and keeping my heart aligned with my Father's goals.

I also wanted to thank all my fans for their support. I appreciate all the emails, letters, encouragement, and love you send my way. It is so great to receive letters from my friends across the United States, Germany, and my friends I have yet to meet in England! I really appreciate all the motivation and hope you bring!

About the Author

   I was born in Baton Rouge, Louisiana and still reside there today. I graduated from Southeastern Louisiana University with a degree in Human Resource Management. Go Lions! I love to travel and Europe is my favorite destination, but if I had to choose one I would say Paris. I enjoy anything adventures, plays, musicals, and concerts. My favorite musicians are Lifehouse, Oak and Gorski (Ken Oak Band), and Final Fantasy. I also enjoy the art of Final Fantasy and it inspired some of my graphics and layouts. I'm also inspired by my favorite authors Akiane and Robert Frost.

My Spirit Will Not Wait for Me

My Father does not forsake me
Here the enemy does not dare trespass
In the darkness of my failure
Still holy standing

Face down only one finds me
No one utters sound in the distance
They don't go where I have been

In silence I hear things I cannot speak
I watch my enemies tremble
Their steps venture carefully

They do not understand
My steps can't match theirs
Neither can my heart move another's

But is it possible for my heart to look like yours?
Do my footsteps follow your footprints?
Does not the same power you possess flow through me?

Endless

"My Father tells me I must wait but He holds me in grace. I know one day this moment will be mine to keep."

They're so young
And they're so sure,
But my mind is empty and void.

Patience has set far behind,
Pushed my faith to the edge,
Violent scars that will not heal.

It hurts me,
Nearly destroys me.
Breaks my trust,
Kills my belief.
Puts me to sleep in this state.

A fire in the sky,
A glimpse of hope;
Probably not for me,
Reminds me where I need to be.

Cold of December

First Christmas without you here,
Seems shorter than a year. I can still
feel the warmth of your hand in mine
and our lips meeting under the mistletoe.

Now without you near, I'll have no
one to cuddle away the cold of
December.

Foggy lights raining white, little red
hat you always forgot. I miss putting
it back on and retrieving what was lost.

Every second you're not in my arms is
every minute that recalls how far you
truly are.

It all gets lost with the distance and I
can only watch, as time falls into the
cold of December.

Thoughts of Finding You

Thoughts of thoughts
Dreaming of dreams
Lies that keep the truth silent
And a heart that can't rediscover.

Shadows that speak
Saying we'll never be,
But I'm willing to get lost
If it means getting lost in you.

This darkness seems to follow me,
Will sunlight come in the end?
• If freedom has been locked away
Could you open what's been closed to me?

"He reacts to my brokenness.....I will pray until He arrives."

The Father's Love

Whispering clouds
Ocean like skies
A greeting light
Followed by a cold night

Unsteady waters
Deliberate in movement
A harsh reminder
Followed by a reviving dawn

Sustained in truth
Filled with love
Tangled in faith
Held with promise

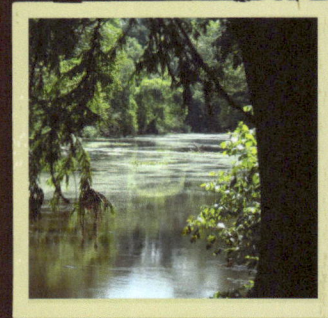

Replenished by His spirit
Delighted by His mystery
Bought by His blood
Forgiven by His mercy

A tomorrow no longer familiar to me
A new path already paved for me
A new life given to me
A father's extravagant love for me

The Calling

"What's important to me is important to God. Therefore what's important to God should be important to me."

Love like no other found
Called to give back what I cannot hold
This grace more than sufficient for me
I desire to give back all that over flows

There is nothing else I long to do
Than make your love known
Your grace over me
And my heart consumed by you

Your breath gave me life
But there is a breathless world in need of you
What part can I play?
For this is the call of my heart

My Favorites

I Wonder

I wonder what it's like to be outside your body,
To feel someone else's pain;
To have thoughts you don't own.

I wonder what its like to be asleep
But can't wake up.
Or be awake
And want to disappear.

I wonder what its like to have unwanted thoughts,
To feel like you have nothing to live for.
Or to be sick and awaiting death,
Getting ready to see God's face.

I wonder what its like to live a life worth reliving,
To feel God resting on the inside;
To feel so undeserving.

I wonder what its like to see your dreams come true,
To see God's plan unfold before you.
To ask if time could go slow
Because it would be too sweet to let it go.

A Placed Reserved for Someone Listening

I've never focused on the stars at night,
How they fill the vast and empty sky.
Somewhere far, far away;
A placed reserved for someone listening.

Though my faith is smaller than it used to be,
I hope it's still the size of a mustard seed.
If quantity is better than quality,
I'm going to pray the night away.

How could I pray for one thing for so long?
Four years is an eternity to me,
All my attempts to bring this simple message to you.

I've been very ill,
No one knows how ill I've been.
I still believe one day you'll heal me.
I try and pray as quiet as I can,
Where only you are quietly listening.

You should see the stars tonight,
How they never fall from their height.
I'm still quietly praying,
To a place reserved for someone listening.

"God is fully responsible for the one who is
fully devoted to Him."

Conversation

I'm not so sure it can work

"I don't think it can, what about the distance"

This will destroy me

"My lips are sealed"

"Will we meet again in New York?"

Give me a sign

Germany?

Wie Gehts? Ich Lerne!

"Gut!"

But...I'm the one making the sacrifice

"I understand"

Our relationship will never be the same

"I know"

"Do you think...we can slow dance tonight?"

I would love that

"We must keep this here"

I gave too much

China?   Paris?

"They can never know "

"Let's run off to Philly"

It's only a flight away

"But...you need to make a decision"

I spent the winter alone in Canada

I miss you   *"I love you"*

How much?

"Your name forever written on my heart"

I will pay more of a price

South Korea?

"Somethings are better left unsaid"

Not meant to be...not meant for me

"But God has to send me someone"

He will send you someone

"I'm not so sure anymore"

I need you

I'm more unsure about you than ever before

"Needless to say...I need you the most"

"What about?" I'm not saying anything

I haven't told them

"You need to let them know"

Burial at Sea

"My scars will never drown."

Hardwood floors
Windows open despite the cold
Knee caps to test their strength
Heart is heavy, eyes haven't slept

Walk quietly through her halls
She can not hear my bare steps
To the streets I retreat
Where the ocean's light is dim

Dump all the remains
Watch it sink into the abyss
Burial at Sea........

Gatekeeper

Gatekeeper of my heart, how locked away is your greatest keepsake? So careful are you, is there anyone you would pass along to? Never ceasing prayer for you to usher such a worthy soul in. How valuable am I to you?

Cautious are your steps; will anyone be allowed to walk in? But how long will I wait? How long until my journey begins? How old will I be? Will I start to grey? Surely my youth will not pass away.

I remain hopeful though patience has been replaced with loneliness. Gracious are your truths and blessed are those who remain true, for my heart still belongs to you.

"I'm filled with crippling doubt."